Sidesplitting Jokes

HA! HA!

CRAZY CRITTERS JOKE BOOK

HA! HA!

HA! HA!

Why don't bears wear shoes?
There's no point, they'd still have bear feet.

Lisa Regan

WINDMILL BOOKS

Published in 2020 by Windmill Books,
an Imprint of Rosen Publishing
29 East 21st Street, New York, NY 10010

Cataloging-in-Publication Data

Names: Regan, Lisa.
Title: Crazy critters joke book / Lisa Regan.
Description: New York : Windmill Books, 2020. | Series: Sidesplitting jokes | Includes glossary and index.
Identifiers: ISBN 9781725395824 (pbk.) | ISBN 9781725395848 (library bound) | ISBN 9781725395831 (6 pack)
Subjects: LCSH: Animals--Juvenile humor. | Wit and humor, Juvenile.
Classification: LCC PN6231.A5 R465 2020 | DDC 808.88'2--dc23

Manufactured in the United States of America

CPSIA Compliance Information: Batch BW20WM: For Further Information contact
Rosen Publishing, New York, New York at 1-800-237-9932

WARNING!

This book is dangerously funny!

Are you ready for the best selection of funny stuff ever gathered together under one cover? Prepare yourself for a heap of brand new jokes, a pile of classic sidesplitters, and a big bundle of laughs. It all adds up to a stack of fun to share with your friends and family. Warn them to find a safe place to listen, as they'll soon be laughing their heads off!

What do you get if you cross a parrot with a centipede?

A walkie-talkie.

Why was the lightning bug unhappy?

Because her children weren't so bright.

Why doesn't a snail get faster without its shell to weigh it down?

It actually becomes more sluggish.

What do you get when you cross a sheep and a honeybee?

Baa humbug.

What do happy frogs say?

Time's fun when you're having flies!

How do you find where a flea has bitten you?

Start from scratch.

What did the dog say to the flea?

Stop bugging me!

What's worse than a centipede with athlete's foot?

A porcupine with split ends.

What happened when the dairy farmers went on strike?

It was udder chaos.

What sport do horses play indoors?

Stable tennis.

How do you fit two sheep on a bicycle?

Put one on the seat and one on the handle-baas.

How do sheep cook their food?

On a baa-baa-cue.

How do cows travel really fast?

On a moo-torbike.

Did you hear about the cow that slept in the henhouse?

It was roost beef.

How do you heat a sheep farm?

Central bleating.

How do you arrest a pig farmer?

Put him in ham cuffs.

Why did the snake cross the road?

To get to the other sssssside!

Why didn't the koala go to college?

It didn't have the right koalafications.

What do you call a snake with no clothes on?

Sss-naked.

Why did the dog cross the road twice?

It was trying to fetch a boomerang.

What's the definition of out-of-bounds?

An exhausted kangaroo.

What do you call a lazy baby kangaroo?

A pouch potato.

Why are snakes hard to play tricks on?

You can't pull their leg.

What do you call a dishonest reptile?

A crookodile.

Why are giraffes the snootiest animals in Africa?

It takes them a long time to swallow their pride.

What did the lion say to the lioness?

Do you want to grab a bite to eat?

How can you make a hippo do whatever you say?

Hippo-notism.

How does a dog stop watching YouTube videos?

It presses the paws button.

Why won't a lion eat you if you tell it a joke?

Because you might taste funny.

What do you call a crocodile with GPS?

A navi-gator!

Why aren't leopards good at hiding?

Because they're always spotted.

What do you call a snake that is 3.14 feet long?

A pi-thon.

How do sheep farmers sign their letters?

Ewes sincerely.

What do you call a herd of sheep rolling down a hill?

A lambslide.

How do you fit more pigs on a farm?

Build a sty-scraper.

Where do sheep go for some sunshine?

The Baa-hamas.

What animal says, "OO"?

A cow with no lips.

What did the mother cow say to her calf?

It's way pasture bedtime.

What horse can't run or jump?

A clotheshorse.

Did you hear about the horse that escaped after dark?

What a night-mare!

What's the difference between a car and a buffalo?

A car only has one horn.

Why did the turkey get arrested?

Fowl play.

Why do bears have fur coats?

They'd look stupid in parkas!

Why don't bears wear shoes?

There's no point, they'd still have bear feet.

How many skunks does it take to make a big stink?

Quite a phew.

What does a daddy buffalo say as his little one goes to school?

Bison!

What's black and white and black and white and black and white and green?

Three skunks fighting over an apple.

Did you give money to that bison farmer?

Yes, but it was just a buffa-loan.

What do polar bears need on hot days?

Bear conditioning.

What's white, furry, and lives in your mouth?

A molar bear!

What do grizzlies eat for dessert?

Blue-BEAR-y pie!

What do polar bears eat for dinner?

Icebergers and chili sauce.

What do you call a bear in the rain?

A drizzly bear.

Why are igloos round?

So polar bears can't hide in the corners.

Why did the grizzly get fired from its job?

It was only doing the bear minimum.

Why didn't the teddy bear eat dessert?

He was stuffed!

What shade should you paint your cat's basket?

Purrrple.

Why are cats good at video games?

Because they have nine lives.

What music do rabbits like best?

Hip-hop.

What do you call a rabbit with fleas?

Bugs bunny.

How does a porcupine play leapfrog?

Very carefully.

What did the dog say when it sat on sandpaper?

Ruff!

What do you call a small dog with a sore throat?

A little husky.

What has six eyes but cannot see?

Three blind mice.

What do you get if you cross a cowboy with an octopus?

Billy the Squid.

What does an oyster do on its birthday?

It shellebrates.

How do crabs call their friends?

On shell phones.

What is the strongest creature on the ocean floor?

A mussel.

What eats animals two by two?

Noah's shark!

What does an octopus wear when it is cold?

A coat of arms.

Did you hear about the killer whale that played violin?

It joined an orca-stra.

How do you make an octopus laugh?

With ten tickles.

What was the first animal in space?

The cow that jumped over the moon.

What do you call the funniest bird on the farm?

A comedi-hen.

What do you call a pig in a car?

A road hog!

When does a horse start to talk?

Whinney wants to.

What do you call a reptile private detective?

An investi-gator.

How does a farmer count his herd?

With a cowculator.

What time does a duck wake up?

At the quack of dawn.

What animal says, "AAB"?

A sheep talking backward.

Glossary

igloo A dome-shaped house built from blocks of snow.

lightning bug A type of beetle that produces light in its body.

mare A female horse.

orca A large, black-and-white killer whale.

parka A jacket with a thick lining and a hood with fur around the edge.

Index